COMMUNICATING WITH **CONFIDENCE**™

NONVERBAL COMMUNICATION
THE ART OF BODY LANGUAGE

LIZ SONNEBORN

ROSEN
PUBLISHING®

New York

Published in 2012 by The Rosen Publishing Group, Inc.
29 East 21st Street, New York, NY 10010

Copyright © 2012 by The Rosen Publishing Group, Inc.

First Edition

Library of Congress Cataloging-in-Publication Data

Sonneborn, Liz.
Nonverbal communication: the art of body language/Liz Sonneborn.
    p. cm.—(Communicating with confidence)
Includes bibliographical references and index.
ISBN 978-1-4488-5518-6 (library binding: alk. paper)—ISBN 978-1-4488-5629-9 (pbk.: alk. paper)—ISBN 978-1-4488-5630-5 (6-pack: alk. paper)
1. Body language—Juvenile literature. 2. Nonverbal communication—Juvenile literature. I. Title.
BF637.N66S66 2012
153.6'9–dc22

                                                             2011006581

Manufactured in the United States of America

CPSIA Compliance Information: Batch #W12YA: For further information, contact Rosen Publishing, New York, New York, at 1-800-237-9932.

CONTENTS

INTRODUCTION

I magine you've been invited to a party thrown by the Nonverbal triplets—Stacy, Tracy, and Lacy. You don't know them personally, but you have plenty of friends in common. And your friends have told you all about the Nonverbal girls.

Stacy is the achiever. She is the editor of your high school newspaper, the head of the debate club, and the student body president. No one was surprised to learn that she won a full scholarship to a prestigious college after wowing its administrators during an interview.

Tracy is the organizer. Whenever your school is holding a bake sale or benefit concert, Tracy Nonverbal is always behind the scenes. She knows how to get things done, but your friends who've worked alongside her say it's hard to be around Tracy for too long. She's just too nervous and anxious about all the things that could go wrong.

Lacy is the loner. She spends most of her time alone or with just a few close friends. Whenever she gets in a crowd, Lacy feels awkward and shy. She would much rather hang around in her room than show up at the party her two sisters insisted they throw.

When you walk into the Nonverbal house, the party is in full swing. You want to introduce yourself

In any conversation, if you stand tall, hold your head high, and make eye contact with the people you're speaking with, you will appear confident and in control.

to your hosts, so you scan the room for Stacy, Tracy, and Lacy. They aren't hard to spot. After all, there are only three girls there with identical facial features. The rest of them look similar as well. All three Nonverbal girls have a medium build, wear their brown hair at shoulder-length, and are dressed in sweaters and jeans. Nothing about them seems to offer even the slightest clue to which triplet is which.

Then you notice something. One of the Nonverbal girls seems distracted, looking around the room even though she's surrounded by her friends. Her brow is furrowed, and her lips are stretched thin. She's twirling a strand of hair with her finger, and she keeps tapping one of her feet. You're getting anxious just looking at her. She's got to be Tracy.

You take a second look at another of the triplets. She's off by herself. Her arms are wrapped around her slumping shoulders, and her eyes are looking down at the floor. She seems so uncomfortable that you're sure she's Lacy.

You figure that the third sister has to be Stacy. But your guess is based on more than just the process of elimination. The third Nonverbal is standing tall, with her shoulders back and her feet planted firmly on the floor. She's fully engaged in the conversation she's having, looking her friends straight in the eye and sometimes reaching out to lightly touch them on the arm when she's trying to make a point. This confident triplet is definitely Stacy.

How did you manage to tell Stacy, Tracy, and Lacy apart even though they appeared identical? You instinctively used your knowledge of body language. When people communicate with others, they all use more than just words. In fact, the expressions on their faces, the gestures they make, and even the way they stand can say much more about them than what comes out of their mouths. This book will help you learn more about body language and how it works. You can use that knowledge not just to understand other people better but also to present yourself to the world in exactly the way you want to be seen.

CHAPTER 1

WHAT IS NONVERBAL COMMUNICATION?

Before early humans developed spoken language, they were still able to communicate with one another. They may not have had words, but they had something just as expressive—facial expressions and body movements that allowed them to "speak" with those around them.

Even after developing language, human beings continued to use movements to express themselves. Experts who study these movements refer to them as nonverbal communication. Most nonscholars simply call them body language. Humans use body language from their earliest moments of life.

Long before they can speak, babies communicate with their parents with their movements and expressions.

Body language involves just about every body part, literally from head to toe. It includes head movements, facial expressions, hand gestures, posture, torso shifts, and positioning of legs and feet. Eye contact, tone of voice, and even the amount of space between people in a conversation are also considered part of nonverbal communication. Whether standing or sitting, as long as some part of your body is in motion, you are communicating through body language.

Studying Nonverbal Communication

In 1872, Charles Darwin, the renowned naturalist who proposed the theory of evolution, published *The Expression of the Emotions in Man and Animals*. Darwin discussed the similarities in facial expressions among humans, apes, and monkeys, all of which, according to his theory, evolved from a common ancestor. For many years, this early study in nonverbal communication remained one of the few scholarly books on the subject. Only in the mid-twentieth century did scholars truly begin taking body language seriously as a subject of study. Nonverbal communication has since been analyzed by experts in many fields, including zoologists, psychologists, and anthropologists.

Among the most important pioneers in the study of body language was anthropologist Ray L. Birdwhistell. By analyzing films of his research subjects, he studied body movements and their meanings, a field he called kinesics. Also instrumental in the study of nonverbal communication were Paul Ekman and W. V.

Scholars have long been interested in facial expressions, as seen by this page from *Science and Society*, published in 1895. The modern study of body language, however, did not begin until the mid-twentieth century.

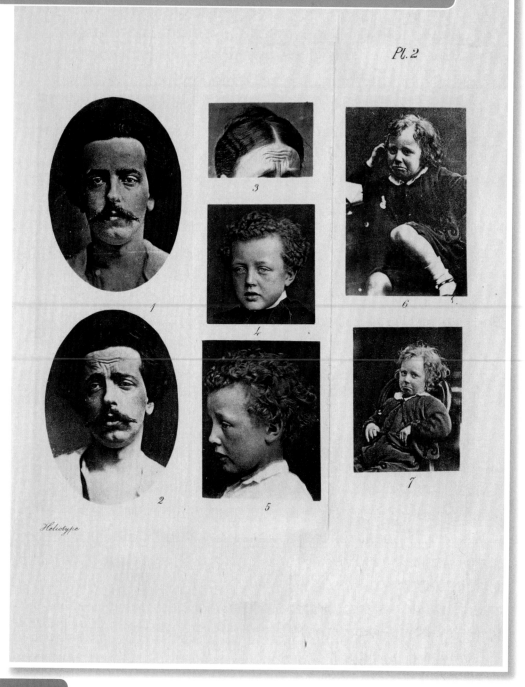

Friesen. They developed the Facial Action Coding System, also called FACS. FACS is a system of analyzing and interpreting even the smallest facial movement. Today, it is used by psychiatrists to diagnose patients who have trouble communicating and by law enforcement officers to get a read on suspects. It is also studied by filmmakers of animated movies who want to make their characters' expressions look as real as possible.

Another important person in the field of nonverbal communication is Albert Mehrabian, who was a professor of psychology at the University of California–Los Angeles and is now retired. His research found that only 7 percent of a message communicated by one person to another comes from the words spoken. He claimed that the tone of voice accounted for 38 percent, while other elements of body language made up a whopping 55 percent. Other experts have questioned these exact percentages. But all agree that body language plays a substantial role in any conversation.

Types of Body Movements

Just what do body movements communicate? In general, while words transmit facts and information, most body language conveys feelings, emotions, and attitude. In addition, communication through body language is almost instant. When you meet strangers, you start forming an opinion about them within seconds, largely because of nonverbal communication.

Experts also know that different types of body movements communicate different types of information. In their research,

Taken together, facial expressions and gestures can send a powerful message. No one could see this girl's downturned eyebrows, tight lips, and clenched hands and think she was feeling anything but anger.

Paul Ekman and W. V. Friesen grouped gestures and other movements into five different categories:

Emblems: These movements take the place of words. For instance, if you purse your lips and place your index finger over your mouth, you are saying, "Be quiet." Or if you wink at someone during a conversation, you are saying, "I'm acknowledging that there is something we both know that we are not saying out loud."

Illustrators: As their name suggests, these movements help illustrate what you are saying. Say you tell someone, "I caught the biggest fish you've ever seen." You might hold out your hands wide apart to help illustrate just how big.

Affective displays: These movements, usually made with the face, are a response to a particular emotion. For example, if you suddenly get really mad, without even thinking about it, your mouth will tighten, your forehead will furrow, and your eyebrows will turn down and in.

Regulators: Regulators help control a conversation. One example is a slow nod. If you're speaking with someone and the person begins nodding, you'll take that as a signal that the person understands you and wants you to continue talking.

Adaptors: These movements help people release nervous tension and relieve anxiety. Rubbing the back of your neck,

Body Language Around the World

People everywhere communicate through body language. But in different cultures, the same gesture or body movement can have different meanings.

For instance, in England and Germany, maintaining eye contact is considered good manners, as it is in the United States. In parts of Africa and Asia, however, it is seen as a sign of disrespect.

Throughout much of the world, nodding suggests you agree with what another person is saying. People in Greece and Turkey, though, interpret nodding in the opposite way. If you nod there, you are saying "no." If you are in the Middle East, take care not to sit with your ankle on your knee. This position exposes the sole of your shoe. Showing someone the bottoms of your feet in Middle Eastern culture is a grievous insult.

Many common hand gestures can also get you into trouble abroad. You might think touching someone on the head is an affectionate gesture. But in many Asian countries, it is considered very rude. In parts of Europe, the standard American hand wave doesn't mean "hello" or "good-bye," but is read as a sign meaning "no." Also, don't congratulate someone in Australia on a job well done with a thumbs-up. An Australian will see this as an obscene gesture.

If you ever plan to travel to a foreign country, you will probably try to learn a little about the language spoken there before you go. Remember, though, that it is just as important to find out about the body language customs in any country you're visiting. Otherwise, you might accidentally confuse or, worse, insult any new friends you make there.

drumming your fingers on a table, and fiddling with jewelry are all adaptors.

Conscious and Subconscious Gestures

You can't control some body language. For instance, feelings of pleasure cause the pupils of your eyes to dilate, or grow larger. It's a matter of biology. No matter how hard you try, you cannot will your pupils not to dilate in this situation.

When you feel certain emotions, your face will also naturally take on corresponding expressions. In one example, when you hear great news, your mouth will spontaneously break out in a smile. But, if you want to hide your feelings from others, you have the ability to consciously pull the corners of your mouth down to give your face a more neutral expression. You can also put on a fake smile in an effort to convince others you're happy when you're not.

Some body movements you make you are hardly aware of. Adaptors often fall into this category. For instance, to comfort yourself in a tense situation, you might chew on your lip. When you start doing this, you don't first think to yourself, "Why, I'm feeling uncomfortable, so I'm going to rub my teeth over my lower lip to make myself feel better." Your decision to chew your lip is made on a purely subconscious level.

On the other hand, some gestures, especially emblems and illustrators, are almost always made consciously. For example, waving good-bye or giving an OK sign with your hand is just as much a conscious act as saying the words "good-bye" or "OK."

By biting her lip, this teenager is subconsciously revealing her feelings of unease and discomfort. Her unwillingness to make eye contact further suggests her anxiety.

Crafting Your Image

You might wonder why you should study nonverbal communication. After all, if you, like everyone else, already uses body language, why do you need to learn about it? There are two especially good reasons.

First, you can teach yourself how to pick up on the signals other people's gestures and expressions are sending. Understanding body language won't turn you into a mind reader who instantly knows what everyone else is secretly thinking. But it might give you clues about how other people are feeling, which might help you communicate with them better.

Second, studying body language can also make you more aware of the signals your body is sending—both consciously and subconsciously. Some people, like many actors and politicians, are naturally good at manipulating their body language to project a certain image. But most people don't have this gift. To improve their body language, they have to work hard to adopt movements that create a positive image and to stop making ones that don't. The rewards, though, are worth the effort. At school, at work, and at home, you'll be able to build better relationships and have greater success once you have learned to use body language to your advantage.

CHAPTER 2

IN YOUR FACE

To understand the importance of your facial expressions, imagine this scenario. Your father had promised to take you to the movies, but now he says he can't. His friend Al called and wants your father to come over right away to help him change a flat tire on his car. Your father keeps saying how sorry and unhappy he is about the sudden change of plans. But you notice, just for a fraction of a second, that the corners of his mouth rise and the skin along his temples wrinkles. Just as soon as you see it, his sly little smile is gone.

Your father has given you mixed signals. His words tell you he's unhappy. But his face, at least for an unguarded instant, tells you he's happy. Which are you more likely to believe? If you are like most people, you would guess that no matter what your dad is saying, secretly he would rather hang out with Al than go to the movies with you. There is a good reason for coming to that conclusion. Facial expressions are so important to human communication that people are much more apt to believe what your face expresses than what you say with words.

Universal Expressions

Often hand gestures mean different things in different countries. For instance, in the United States, holding up your hand with your index finger and thumb forming an O-shape means "OK." In Brazil, on the other hand, the same gesture is considered very obscene.

Facial expressions, though, are different. According to the research of psychologist and body language expert Paul Ekman, there are six universal emotions that are expressed through the muscles of the face. Ekman holds that the facial expressions that accompany these emotions are the same with people the world over:

Anger: Eyebrows pull down and in, forehead wrinkles, nostrils flare, lips tighten

Disgust: Eyebrows lower, nose wrinkles, upper lip raises

Lowered eyebrows, a wrinkled nose, and a raised upper lip all betray feelings of disgust, one of the six universal emotions that are communicated with the same facial expressions by people around the world.

Fear: Eyebrows raise, eyelids open, corners of mouth stretch back

Happiness: Eyes narrow, skin near eyes wrinkles, corners of lips raise, lips separate

Sadness: Inner end of eyebrows raise, eyelids lower, corners of lips lower

Surprise: Eyebrows raise, eyelids open, mouth opens

(Ekman later concluded that contempt—expressed by a half smile on one side of the mouth—is a seventh universal emotion, although some scholars are not convinced that this emotion is recognized by all people.)

Whenever you feel one of these emotions, your features will automatically move into the corresponding expression. Of course, you can fight that impulse. Everyone knows what it's like to try to look happy when you're sad or to try to hide that you're afraid.

Faking an expression, however, is not always easy. No matter how hard you work at controlling your facial muscles, they sometimes momentarily slip into the expression that reveals your true feelings. These are called microexpressions.

Being aware of microexpressions can help you realize if someone is trying to mask their feelings. Also keep in mind, when someone is faking an emotion, they often get the appropriate facial expression slightly wrong. Fake happiness is especially easy to spot. When people put on a fake smile, they

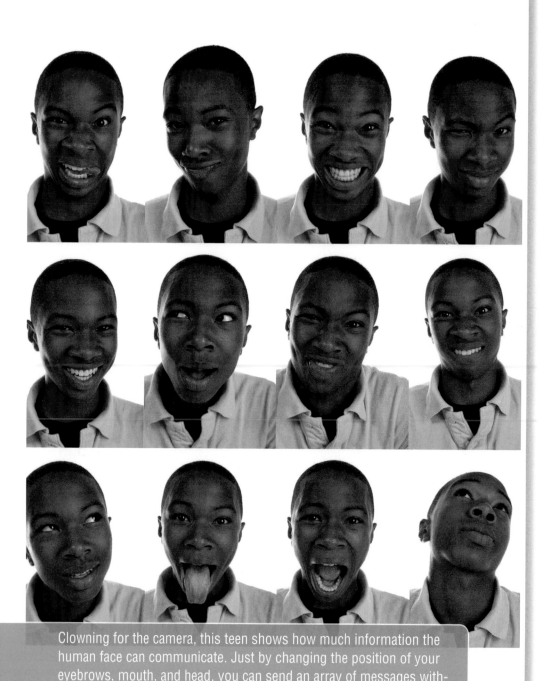

Clowning for the camera, this teen shows how much information the human face can communicate. Just by changing the position of your eyebrows, mouth, and head, you can send an array of messages without saying a word.

often use only the bottom half of their face. The skin on the outer edge of their eyes doesn't crinkle like it does when a person is smiling sincerely.

Lips and Eyes

Even though real happiness always inspires a smile, not all smiles convey the same meaning. A tight-lipped smile suggests that you might be trying to keep something to yourself. A lopsided smile makes you look as though you aren't entirely happy. You might wear one after making a silly mistake, like tripping over your own feet. It would signal that, even though you're amused by your misstep, you also feel embarrassed. A wide smile can be inviting, but an overly big one makes you seem too eager to please.

Lips give away your emotions in other ways as well. If you're relaxed, you hold your lips loosely. But if you're tense or anxious, they naturally stretch tight. People also often tighten their lips when they are trying to hide sadness or anger. A sudden puckering of the lips usually signals that someone disagrees with what you're saying. People also sometimes reveal their disapproval by touching their lips.

Even more revealing than your mouth are your eyes. When you are happy or excited, your eyes seem to sparkle with energy. When you are sad or bored, they appear dull and blank.

You have probably heard that you should make eye contact with people you are speaking with. Certainly, eye contact builds a bond between people, so it is helpful if you are trying to get someone to focus on what you have to say. But too

Making Your Voice Heard

Many body language experts consider the human voice to be part of nonverbal communication—not the words it speaks, but the messages its tone conveys. You might have had to sit through lectures by teachers who speak entirely in a monotone. Even if what they had to say was fascinating, you probably didn't notice. An unchanging tone is so boring that listeners tend to tune out.

Another common problem is speaking too fast or slow. Either one sounds unnatural and is therefore off-putting. Some speakers also do not modulate their voices properly. If you speak too softly, you come across as weak, but if you speak too loudly, you appear aggressive. Instead, strive to speak at a normal rate and volume. Take care to insert short pauses after each phrase and longer pauses at the end of each sentence.

To be an effective speaker, also avoid the verbal pause. When you use a verbal pause, instead of injecting a brief silence after a phrase, you insert a stand-in word or noise, such as "um," "ah," "like," or the dreaded "you know." People addicted to a verbal pause usually don't even realize what they are saying, but listeners certainly do. Overusing verbal pauses is not just annoying. It also makes you appear not confident and even a little stupid.

To find out if you have a problem with verbal pauses, listen to videos or audiotapes of yourself talking. (Voice mail messages are especially useful in diagnosing the problem.) If you hear a string of "ahs" and "you knows," start training yourself to replace them with brief silent pauses.

much eye contact is just as bad as too little. Too little will make you appear uninterested in the other person. But too much will make you seem angry and aggressive.

If you're shy, maintaining proper eye contact can be difficult. But with practice, you can make yourself more comfortable with it. When speaking with close friends, practice looking directly into their eyes. In more formal conversations, it might be less intimidating for you to look slightly higher up. Picture a triangle on the other person's face, with its top point in the middle of the forehead and its base as a line connecting the two eyes. Try centering your gaze in the middle of this triangle.

Heads Up

In conversations, there's more going on above the neck than just facial expressions. Your head itself can help you both get someone's attention and say what you mean.

The word "tête-à-tête" suggests the importance of head position in communication. In French, *tête-à-tête* literally means "head to head." The word is used to describe a close private conversation. You've probably noticed that people in a tête-à-tête really do hold their heads close to one another. This head position increases the intimacy between people and sends the signal that they do not want to be interrupted.

Another way to show someone you're interested in what he or she is saying is the head tilt. By just slightly tilting your head to one side, you can assure other people that they have your ear. Tilting your head backward with your chin jutting forward is a much less friendly gesture. It suggests you are snooty and

People in intimate conversations often speak with their heads very close together. Even though these girls' heads are close, their lack of eye contact reveals that they're open to others joining them.

arrogant. Tilting your head with your chin close to your chest conveys the opposite message. It says you are weak and submissive.

Holding your head with your hands does not present a strong image. Subconsciously, you are trying to protect your head, one of your most vulnerable body parts, by making a hand helmet. Watch out, too, for rubbing the back of your neck with your hands. Again, this gesture subtly signals weakness for similar reasons.

During a class or lecture, people often rest their chins in one of their hands. The gesture makes them look extremely bored and tired— so much so that if someone grabbed their hand away, you would expect their heads to simply flop forward. If you want others to think they have your full attention, this is probably the worst gesture you can make. But, as with many aspects of body language, reading head-to-hand contact is not always so simple. If your eyes are bright and focused, lightly resting your hand on your cheek can actually make you look as though you're thinking long and hard about your companion's words.

MYTHS
and

MYTH: People who don't make eye contact in conversation are lying.

Fact: It's a common misconception that liars are unable to maintain eye contact—so common that many people go out of their way to stare into others' eyes when they are telling their most bald-faced lies. (As a result, too much eye contact can sometimes be a tip-off that someone's not being completely straight with you.) In fact, many people might not look you in the eye for reasons that have nothing to do with what they are saying. Very often, they are simply shy or uncomfortable in social situations.

MYTH: When you meet someone, you should always wear a big smile on your face.

Fact: When you smile, people are likely to think you're pleasant and approachable. But in more formal situations, people can interpret smiling as a form of weakness. When one person in a group smiles while everyone else is wearing a more neutral expression, the smiler will be seen as the person with the least power. If you're in a situation in which you want to appear serious and capable, such as a job interview, it's probably best to avoid smiling too broadly.

facts

MYTH: A single gesture can tell you all you need to know about how someone is feeling.

Fact: Self-touching gestures, like rubbing the back of the neck, can mean that a person is anxious. But then again, maybe it just means the person has a sore neck. As this example suggests, trying to read what someone is thinking and feeling through body language is tricky. Don't draw conclusions from a single gesture. Instead, you should study the entire body to see if it's sending you a complete message. If the neck rubber at other times is drumming his fingers on a table and twirling his foot around in circles, you can assume that he's feeling pretty uncomfortable. But if other than the neck rub, he seems calm and collected, maybe you were jumping to conclusions when you decided he had a bad case of nerves.

Think of each element of body language as a word. Words alone don't mean much. But when you put them together into sentences and paragraphs, they can begin to tell you a story.

A SHOW OF HANDS

f you want to understand the importance of hand gestures, try this experiment. Attempt to describe to a friend an action sequence in one of your favorite movies without using your hands. Likely, you will soon realize just how hard it is. In conversation, people tend to use their hands to explain and emphasize their words far more than they realize. In fact, aside from your face, your hands play the most important role in nonverbal communication.

Hiding and Protecting

Understandably, people who hide their hands in their pockets appear to be

With his head down, shoulders slumped, and hands firmly thrust into his pockets, this teen makes it clear that he is not interested in talking with anybody around him.

uncommunicative. Your hands are such important communicators that, if you obscure them from view, you look as though you are withholding information. Out of nervousness or just out of habit, many people pocket their hands without realizing that they are handicapping themselves by appearing standoffish and aloof.

Another hand position that can seem off-putting is what some body language experts call the fig leaf pose. In this position, the hands are clasped together and placed in front of the crotch area. This pose is so common that many people think nothing of it. But on a subconscious level, it sends a message. Humans, for good reason, regard their crotch as a vulnerable area. Without thinking about it, they naturally try to protect it. In the case of the fig leaf pose, the hands create a barrier between a person's crotch and other people, a protective maneuver that others sense as evidence of fear and weakness. If you want to appear strong and confident, clasp your hands behind your back or, better yet, place them at your sides. This pose leaves your sensitive crotch area exposed, which your audience will read as a show of strength.

If you really want to exude confidence, you might try hooking your thumbs on your belt or pants pocket. Humans see thumbs as vulnerable body parts, so by brazenly displaying them, you show that you are unafraid and in charge. The move can come off as a little macho and even aggressive, however. If you sense people are uncomfortable by your thumb display, you should probably put your hands back down at your sides.

Making Your Point

While talking with each other, people often use hand gestures to emphasize a point. One such gesture is the steeple, in which

This girl is getting her audience's attention through her forceful use of body language. Her gesture, which makes her hands look as though they are holding an imaginary ball, helps her emphasize the point she's making.

people place the fingertips of both hands together to form an upside-down V-shape. Used sparingly, the steeple can make you seem like you know what you're talking about. But too much steepling is a turn-off. People might think you are arrogant and overconfident.

A more effective gesture positions the hands a slight distance apart in front of the body, as though they are holding

A light touch on the shoulder or arm can communicate caring and sympathy. But keep in mind that some people dislike being touched, especially by those they don't know very well.

an imaginary ball. Moving your hands up and down a few times in this position helps signal people to pay special attention to what you are saying without making you look like a know-it-all.

To make the imaginary-ball move a more welcoming gesture, move your hands slightly outward to expose your palms. An open-palm gesture makes you seem forthright and honest. If you're trying to convince someone of your sincerity, an open palm can help.

A palms-down gesture has the opposite effect and can help you cut off a conversation. Think about trying to quiet a room of noisy kids. Although it might not be as effective as yelling "Shut up!," a stern palms-down gesture might be enough to get the less boisterous ones to stop talking.

In Touch

In American society, handshakes are an appropriate and sometimes mandatory touching gesture. But other touching is far less universally acceptable. If you mis-speak with your body language, probably the worst way to do it is through an inappropriate touch.

As an example, imagine there is a kid named David who has just been assigned a new chemistry lab partner, Amy. David meets Amy after school to talk about a lab report that is due in a few days. In the middle of the conversation, Amy suddenly starts crying. David asks her what's the matter, and she says her boyfriend just broke up with her. Without thinking, David puts his hand on her shoulder. Amy bolts up, holds her hands up to create a barrier between them, and yells, "What are you doing?"

What went wrong? Well, just about everything that could, all because of a little touch. Touching is a natural way for a person to provide another with comfort and support. But it is best reserved for people who know each other well. Otherwise, it can quickly be misinterpreted. David was just trying to make Amy feel better, and she might have welcomed his touch if they had been longtime friends. But Amy barely knew David, so she jumped to the conclusion that he was coming on to her and was repelled by his gesture.

David's mistake brings up another problem with touching. Between males and females, even just a small, friendly touch might be misconstrued as a sexual advance. In school or on the job, therefore, you should refrain from touching anyone of the opposite sex. An inappropriate touch might lead to more than a socially awkward moment. It might also get you suspended or fired.

For some people, stopping the impulse to touch others is hard. You may have grown up in a family where kind gestures, such as hugging and putting an arm around another's shoulder, were an important way of communicating love and camaraderie. Keep in mind, though, that others come from families in which people rarely showed affection physically. Still other people just naturally feel uncomfortable about touching, even touching those closest to them. A safe rule is, if in doubt, keep your hands to yourself.

Hair twirling is just one example of self-touching. To relieve anxiety or to release nervous energy, many people compulsively use self-touching gestures, often without realizing what they're doing.

Easing Anxiety

Many touching gestures are adaptors. These involve people touching parts of their own bodies. Examples include running your fingers through your hair, rubbing the back of your neck, stroking your arms, touching your nose, and twirling your hair. People unconsciously use self-touching to comfort themselves when they feel nervous or unsettled.

There are also many other related gestures that involve playing with an object with your hands or mouth. Chances are, you know plenty of people who indulge in these gestures without thinking. Everywhere you look there are change jigglers, jewelry fiddlers, pen chewers, and cigarette smokers. Like self-touching, these activities help people release nervous energy and therefore make them feel less anxious.

It is hard to stop making these gestures. For many people, they are longstanding habits, often ones they are barely aware of. But even if they do not notice them, other people do. In addition to how annoying and distracting the constant fiddling and fidgeting is, it also signals an overall unease. You may think you're projecting an image of a confident, competent person, but if you can't stop drumming a table with your fingertips, people will only see an anxious person desperately trying to make themselves feel in control. No matter what the rest of your body language says, these kinds of gestures will broadcast the insecurity hiding behind the confident pose.

BODY TALK

People analyzing body language often focus on the face and hands. But don't forget that the rest of your body also tells its own story. In addition, sometimes what your body says is something far different from what your face and hands indicate. Many people who are highly skilled at putting on the right expression and making effective hand gestures forget about what their arms, legs, feet, and torso are doing. If you make this mistake, you might confuse your audience or even undermine your intended message.

Arms and Shoulders

The wrong upper body pose can project both vulnerability and incompetence.

CHAPTER 4

Consider one common posture—the shrug. Shruggers hunch their shoulders, a movement unconsciously meant to protect your neck, signaling that the shrugger is reacting to a real or imagined threat. A full shrug—with arms out, palms up, mouth corners lowered, and raised eyebrows—tells others that you are shirking responsibility, that you want no part of what's going on around you.

Crossing your arms in front of your chest is another off-putting posture. By doing so, you make your arms a physical barrier between you and others. Crossed arms say that you are closed off and have little desire to communicate. The gesture is likely to make you seem unapproachable and unfriendly.

In *The Definitive Book of Body Language*, authors Allan and Barbara Pease recount a nonverbal communication experiment that explored the psychological effects of crossing your arms. Researchers gathered a group of volunteers to attend a series of lectures. They told half the volunteers to sit with their arms crossed in front of their chests. They instructed the other half to sit with their arms relaxed. The volunteers with crossed arms retained 38 percent less of the information conveyed in the lectures than those who listened with their arms open. These results suggest that the very act of crossing your arms can actually make you less interested in and receptive to the world around you.

If you want to give the impression that you are an open and forthright person, it is best to sit with your arms open and to stand with your arms relaxed at your sides. Another confident standing pose is to position your hands on your hips. This is

Even if you ignored this teen's angry expression, his crossed arms would still signal that he didn't want to speak with you. By crossing their arms, people subconsciously create a barrier between themselves and others.

sometimes called the Superman pose. It suggests that, just like Superman, you are ready to jump into action. But be aware: the Superman pose is hard to pull off. If you do it half-heartedly, you're more likely to look silly than heroic.

Looking at Legs

Even below the waist, your body language counts. Your leg position, for instance, can make you appear weak or strong. When you're standing, think about whether you would be easy to knock over. Weak positions include a stance with your legs and feet firmly pressed together or a scissored leg position with one leg crossing in front of the other. In either case, one small shove would be enough to land you on the ground. Contrast these with a firm stance, in which you separate your feet by a few inches and distribute your weight evenly on both of them. This feet and leg position will make you seem like

a powerful person, one who is literally able to stand his or her ground.

When sitting, some people, especially women, cross their ankles. They might think the pose makes them look polite and friendly. But, by making the sitter look small, crossed ankles

In this group, the girl at the far right looks like the natural leader. Her wide stance and thumb display make her seem powerful. Her slouching companions, especially the boy with his hands in his pockets, appear far less confident.

actually suggest a person is weak, afraid, and maybe even apologetic—hardly the image most people want to project.

On the other end of the spectrum is the figure-four leg position, in which one ankle rests on the knee of the other leg. Because of the jutting foot and the exposure of the crotch area, this stance makes a person seem in control and in charge. But, for many people, the stance can seem too aggressive. Sitting in a figure-four position, you might risk making people perceive you as an arrogant jerk. For a more neutral, yet powerful, leg position, place your feet slightly apart and firmly on the floor.

Showing Interest

Even very composed people sometimes forget about their feet. They may have complete control over their facial expressions and hand gestures, while their feet are frantically tapping or twitching around in circles. If you are constantly moving your feet, your audience is likely to think that you are nervous and impatient no matter how confident the rest of you seems.

Another thing most people pay little attention to is the direction of their feet. Usually, people unconsciously point their feet toward whoever is of the most interest to them. Imagine you are sitting between two friends. Your face is turned toward your

This pair displays the power of the belly button rule. By positioning their torsos so that they directly face each other, both are signaling that they are very absorbed in this conversation.

friend on the right, but your feet are turned to your friend on the left. You might have inadvertently told your friend on the right that you're much more interested in what your other friend has to say.

Personal Space

In 1966, anthropologist Edward T. Hall in his groundbreaking book *The Hidden Dimension* discussed his theories about proxemics, the study of how humans move through space. He argued that people provide clues about their relationships through how much space they put between themselves and others.

According to Hall, there are five levels of distance between people. The smallest distance is close intimate, reserved for a person's most intimate friends and relatives. Next is intimate, used for close friends, followed by personal, used for people with whom you're having conversations. The social level is appropriate for speaking with strangers, salespeople, and others you don't know well. The largest distance is public, which is employed in public settings. This distance would be used between a speaker and an audience.

Hall's work also led to the concept of personal space. At all times, people maintain a bubble of space around them. If another person intrudes into this personal space, people feel extremely uncomfortable. The amount of personal space people prefer, however, is not the same everywhere, but instead differs from culture to culture. For instance, in the United States, people generally need about 7 to 10 inches (18 to 25 centimeters) of personal space. In many European countries, though, people require less. As a result, Americans in Europe can find themselves feeling discomforted when, in casual conversations, they sense their accustomed personal space being violated.

The research of body expert Albert Mehrabian uncovered a related phenomenon. According to Mehrabian, you instinctively position your torso so that your belly button points to the person of most interest to you. You can use the belly button rule to assure others that you're interested in what they are saying. Just adjust your body so that your belly button is facing square in their direction. You can also use belly button direction to show you're tired of speaking with someone. Just move your torso at an angle away from them, even as you keep your eyes trained on theirs. Most people will get the hint that the conversation is over.

Another important way of showing interest is to lean forward toward the person you are speaking with. Of course, be careful not to move in too close. A close lean is likely to make anyone other than your boyfriend or girlfriend extremely uncomfortable. By the same token, leaning away from someone by slumping in your chair can help break the connection with someone else and show you're no longer interested in speaking with him or her.

Standing Tall

Imagine that your school is holding an assembly to present two candidates for student body president. The first walks slowly to the microphone to deliver a speech to convince you to give her your vote. Her body is slouched, her shoulders are hunched, and her head is drooping so low that her chin nearly touches her chest. When her speech is over, the second candidate steps onto the stage. She moves swiftly and with purpose. Her back

When speaking to a group, be sure to establish eye contact with your audience as soon as possible. The earlier you make this connection, the more likely you will hold your listeners' attention throughout your speech.

is straight, her shoulders are back, and her head is held high.

Who would you vote for? You probably said candidate number two. From the stance of her body alone, she signaled that she was competent, confident, and determined. She appeared much more able to take on the job of president than the first candidate, whose body seemed to say she was tired, weak, and uncomfortable. Of course, if the first candidate's speech was terrific and the second candidate's speech was terrible, you might just forget about body language and vote for candidate number one. Still, with her awful posture, the first candidate did herself a great disservice. Even if she were more qualified and more articulate, many voters would be unable to block out of their minds how poorly she had presented herself.

If you want success in life, do yourself a favor and model the stance and walk of the second candidate. She opened up her entire body, which made her look fearless. Her opponent closed her body off, which signaled that she was afraid of something. Seeing a fearful person makes others feel afraid. But seeing a fearless person makes them feel that they, too, can conquer the world. Everyone gravitates to someone who appears confident for one simple reason—that person makes others feel confident, too.

10 Great Questions
TO ASK YOUR TEACHER

1. What is nonverbal communication (also known as body language)?

2. How important is body language in human communication?

3. Have people always used body language?

4. Do gestures and expressions differ around the world?

5. Does a single gesture always have the same meaning?

6. Is it possible for people to change their everyday body language?

7. Can body language reveal that someone is lying?

8. How can you use gestures to emphasize specific points in conversation?

9. How can nonverbal communication help you make a good first impression?

10. How can you best project confidence through body language?

CHAPTER 5

PUTTING YOUR BEST FACE (AND BODY) FORWARD

Learning about nonverbal communication will quickly make you start looking at other people differently. Maybe you notice that every time your mom fiddles with her wedding ring, she's signaling that she has some kind of problem on her mind. Maybe you see that your favorite teacher is a good speaker largely because of the way he uses hand

Reading Other People

Many people who want to study body language have a particular goal in mind. They aren't very interested in looking at themselves and what their own gestures and movements say to others. They just want to learn how to read the body language of other people.

Reading other people's body language, however, is fairly hard. One gesture doesn't have a single meaning. If a person's hands are tightly wrapped around his or her arms, it could signal that the person is closed off and not interested in having a conversation. Or it could simply mean the person is cold.

If you want to read people, try to study their body movements for about ten minutes when they appear to be calm and content. Note the various movements they make. Don't look at just their face; look at their head, shoulders, hands, and feet. Taken together, any patterns you see constitute a baseline. The baseline is essentially a collection of the various ticks that are natural to the person you're studying.

If you want a window into what a person is thinking, pay attention to any deviations from the baseline. Consider this example: you've been called into the principal's office. He's asking you a lot of questions about your friends, and you don't really know what he's driving at. You notice that the principal normally sits leaning back in his chair. But at one point when you're talking, he leans forward. That deviation suggests that whatever you were saying at that particular moment is the information he was fishing for.

gestures to get his message across. Maybe you realize that your best friend is popular in part because her open body posture puts everyone at ease.

But there is even more that an understanding of body language can do for you. Aside from helping you read other people, it can also give you an invaluable tool for communicating with them. By taking control of your own body language, you can build better relationships with others and project the best possible image of yourself to the world.

Understanding Yourself

To begin using body language more consciously and effectively, you first have to take a close look at yourself. All your life you have been communicating with expressions, gestures, and stances. Only by figuring out how you've been using body language in the past can you decide how to use it better in the future.

Start by thinking about how you come across in conversation. When you're speaking with someone, notice changes in their attention. If another person starts tuning you out, take a moment to think about what your body is doing. Are you self-touching or gesturing in a way that is making them uncomfortable? If, instead, a person seems suddenly more interested in what you are saying, ask yourself if there's something you're doing with your body that is inviting this new attentiveness.

Close friends might also be able to help you. Ask them if they've noticed any peculiarities about your body language. Are there any movements or gestures you routinely make that

To get a read on your own body language, ask a friend with a video camera to film you while you two talk. The video might reveal gestures you commonly make but are not consciously aware of.

are off-putting? If they tell you that your constant finger drumming is annoying or that your steeple hands make you seem pretentious, don't get mad. Instead, focus on changing your bad habits.

Knowing how to shake hands with confidence is an important skill. It can help you earn the respect of bosses, teachers, and other people in positions of authority throughout your life.

Another way to learn about your baseline body language is by looking at videos of yourself. You can even ask a friend to film you in conversation. To get a good read, be sure the conversation is long enough that you forget about the camera and

fall into your old, familiar ways of holding your body.

A mirror can also help you evaluate your nonverbal communication. Stand before a full-length mirror and close your eyes. Think about a time you felt nervous or afraid. Open your eyes, and examine your body and your expression. Close your eyes again, and think about a time you felt confident and in control. Then open your eyes, and take note of how your body language has changed.

Shedding Bad Habits

Through this self-evaluation, you will probably discover some bad gesturing habits. You'll likely find these difficult to break, but it is possible.

If, for instance, you compulsively rub your earlobe whenever you feel antsy, stop doing it immediately whenever you start. Because it's easy not to notice habitual gestures, enlist your friends' help. Tell them to point it out whenever you reach for your lobe. You'll soon get so sick of their alerts that you'll work even harder to get rid of the habit forever.

You can also reduce the impact of your negative body language by changing your environment. If you always shove your hands into your pockets, try wearing clothes without them. If you tend to twitch your feet when you're nervous, try holding important discussions at a table so that no one can see them. If you have trouble sitting up tall, choose chairs with high rigid backs that force you to straighten up.

Changing Your Body Movements

If you really want to develop your body language, you need to do more than just break old bad habits. You need to cultivate new ones that are good. Doing so can be tricky, though. You don't want to adopt new gestures and use them for every occasion. If overnight, you began punctuating everything you say with steeple hands, your friends will likely start looking at you strangely. Instead of being impressed, they will probably be baffled by your new and constant robotlike gesturing.

It's better to take it slow and experiment. Try using steeple hands once to emphasize an important point in a conversation. Think about whether it feels natural to you. More important, check the reaction of the people you're talking with. Did they look confused by the gesture? Or did it help increase their interest in your words?

When you're alone, you can also try out new movements. Stand before a mirror and see how much more confident you look when you stand tall, pull your shoulders back, and position your weight evenly on both feet. Another useful tool is visualization. Close your eyes and imagine yourself making a certain gesture or standing a certain way. Just seeing a movement in your head will help it seem like something you might naturally do.

Take some time, too, to observe the body language of celebrities and other famous people you admire. Note the way they hold their bodies and gesture during interviews, then try the same moves in front of a mirror. You might feel a little stupid, but then again you might find some of the movements that draw you to these people feel natural to you as well.

Adopting new body language will be difficult at first. Because you're gesturing consciously instead of subconsciously as before, it will probably feel odd. But with some practice, you will become comfortable using new gestures. In time, they may even become second nature to you.

Creating Rapport

If you want to improve your body language in social interactions, you first have to ask yourself a question: what goal do I want my body language to achieve?

In many situations, the answer is simple. You want your body language to help create rapport with the person you are talking with. Rapport is a connection between people in which everyone feels that they are being heard, understood,

With eye contact and a smile, this teen is establishing rapport with her friend. By displaying her hands, a vulnerable body part, she also sends the message that she trusts the guy she's speaking with.

and respected. If you are good at achieving rapport with others, you're likely to be a success in life. It's a talent that makes people want to know and work with you.

Central to creating rapport is making a good first impression. When you are introduced to people, shake hands if appropriate and, after they've said their name, repeat it. When people hear others say their name, they immediately feel a bond with them.

Early in your conversation, try to get a read on other peoples' energy level and then match it. If they're excited, you should be excited. If they're calm, you should be calm, too.

Body language experts also recommend mimicking the gestures of the person you're talking to. Seeing one's own gestures repeated is comforting. It also subtly suggests that you and the other person are on the same wavelength. Of course, if you take the mimicking too far, this body language strategy will backfire. Other people will think you are making fun of them, which will immediately, and probably permanently, destroy any rapport you've been able to build.

Be sure, too, to maintain steady but not constant eye contact. Try to sit so that you're on or below other people's eye level. If your face is above their eye level, they will feel as though you're looking down on them.

Once the conversation gets going, slightly leaning toward others will signal that you're interested in what they are saying. Also remember the belly button rule: position your body so that it is directly in front of the people you're speaking with.

When a person says something you agree with, a firm, single nod will show that you think both of you are on the same

When coupled with the appropriate expression, leaning forward and making extended eye contact can be an effective way of communicating anger and distrust.

page. Avoid a series of rapid nods. They might make other people think you want them to stop talking so that you can take over the conversation.

Getting Serious

Sometimes your goal in a conversation is to convince others that you are a serious, competent person. For instance, you might want to make a case to your parents that you can be trusted to stay at home alone for a weekend while they are away. Of course, in all college and job interviews, giving this impression is just as, if not more, important as anything you've written on your application.

To make yourself appear competent and confident, above all you should stand tall with your head up and shoulders back. When you sit, be sure to maintain this open posture. Keeping your arms and hands visible will help make you seem forthright. Before an interview, you might want to sit in a chair in front of a mirror and practice this seated pose.

In a formal conversation, be careful about self-touching gestures, which will immediately betray any nervousness you're feeling. Also, try not to make any gesture unless it has a concrete purpose, such as emphasizing a point. In general, use as few gestures as possible. Too much gesturing can make you seem flighty instead of commanding.

Usually in an interview situation, you do not have much choice about where to sit. But if you do, avoid soft chairs or sofas. They make it too easy for your body to sink down, making you seem small and powerless. If you have to sit in a soft chair, sit slightly on the edge and maintain a straight back.

Creating a confident image is also important when you're called on to make a speech or presentation, whether in front of a class or an auditorium full of people. Force yourself early on to make eye contact with people in the audience. If you don't make that early eye contact, you run the risk of losing their attention for the entire presentation. Simple, direct open-palm hand gestures can help you make the audience concentrate on specific points. But take care not to bring your hands above your chin, or your gesturing will seem more like flailing.

Never point at the audience to emphasize an idea. Most people hate being on the receiving end of this gesture. Nothing will make an audience tune out or even turn on you faster than a pointing finger.

Getting Out of a Bad Situation

Another day-to-day use of body language is to get you out of a bad situation. If you want to end a conversation, you can use the belly button rule and shift your torso so that it doesn't face the person you no longer want to speak with. You can also use belly button position to show your displeasure with someone in the middle of a conversation. For example, if you suddenly think someone is lying to you, shift your belly button away from that individual. That break in intimacy might make the other person nervous enough to tell the truth. If the person

During an important conversation, avoid sitting in a chair with a seat lower than that of the other person. If your eye level is lower, the person will automatically perceive you as weaker and less competent.

does, you can reward him or her by shifting your torso back as a show of trust.

Reducing your eye contact can also send the message that you want a conversation to end. Increasing your eye contact can be a useful tool as well. If you are angry with someone and want him or her to know it without raising your voice, hold your eye contact longer than you normally would. Holding a gaze just a little bit longer can also help you emphasize a point. This makes it clear that you want the other person to take the words you've just spoken very seriously.

Remember that, in general, an open posture (head up, shoulders back, back straight) makes you look powerful and a closed posture (head down, shoulders hunched, back slumped) makes you look powerless. Sometimes, you can use this knowledge to get out of danger. Say you are on a dark street, and you see a menacing figure coming toward you. Standing tall in an open posture and striding purposefully forward might dissuade a potential assailant from attacking you. The same posture, though, might be seen as a challenge by a person who is very angry and looking for a fight. In this situation, it would probably be smart to avert your eyes and adopt a closed posture until the person calms down.

Being the Best You

If you practice open and closed postures, you will probably notice something strange. In an open posture, you not only look strong, but also feel strong. In a closed posture, you not only look weak, but also feel weak.

This reveals what can be so powerful about learning to control your body language. While working to change others' impressions of you, you will also change your impression of yourself. Whenever you feel insecure, adopt an open pose and see what happens. Instantly, you'll feel more confident as well as look more confident.

This fake-it-until-you-make-it approach can help you develop the confidence you need to achieve what you want most in life. As you appear more at ease and in control, you will earn the respect of other people. And as you get more respect, you will become surer of yourself, your skills, and your abilities. Soon enough, you will not just be acting like a confident, powerful person. You will genuinely become one, too.

GLOSSARY

ADAPTOR A body movement that helps people release nervous energy and relieve anxiety.

AFFECTIVE DISPLAY A body movement made in response to a particular emotion.

ANTHROPOLOGIST A person who studies how human cultures developed.

BASELINE A starting point that is later used as a point of comparison.

BODY LANGUAGE Communication through conscious or subconscious hand gestures, facial expressions, and other body movements; also called nonverbal communication.

EMBLEM A body movement that takes the place of words.

EYE CONTACT The act of looking into another person's eyes.

FACIAL EXPRESSION The positioning of facial features that signals a specific emotion.

GESTURE The movement of a part of the body, especially the hands, that expresses a certain meaning.

ILLUSTRATOR A body movement that helps show something said in words.

KINESICS The study of body language and its meaning, pioneered by anthropologist Ray L. Birdwhistell.

MANIPULATE To influence another person's thoughts or behavior.

MICROEXPRESSION A momentary facial expression that reveals the true emotion a person is trying to hide.

MODULATE To vary the tone and strength of one's voice.

NATURALIST A scholar who studies the natural world.

NONVERBAL COMMUNICATION Communication through conscious or subconscious hand gestures, facial expressions, and other body movements; also called body language.

PERSONAL SPACE The minimal amount of physical space between a person and others needed by that person to feel comfortable.

PROXEMICS The study of personal space.

RAPPORT A sense of comfort, familiarity, and understanding in a relationship between people.

REGULATOR A body movement that controls the flow of a conversation.

SELF-TOUCHING GESTURE A gesture in which one part of the body touches another to give a person a feeling of comfort.

STANCE The way a person stands.

SUBCONSCIOUS The part of the mind that influences people's thoughts or actions without their awareness.

TÊTE-À-TÊTE Close conversation between two people, from the French phrase meaning "head to head."

VERBAL PAUSE A word or sound that is inserted in conversation in place of a natural silent pause.

VISUALIZATION The act of imagining an outcome in an effort to bring about that outcome.

VULNERABLE Open to physical harm or emotional hurt.

FOR MORE INFORMATION

Berkeley Psychophysiology Lab
Institute of Personality and Social Research
University of California–Berkeley
4143 Tolman Hall
Berkeley, CA 94720
(510) 643-8952
Web site: http://ist-socrates.berkeley.edu/~ucbpl
In its research into human emotions, the Berkeley Psychophysiology
    Lab analyzes the movement of facial muscles responsible for
    expressions.

Canadian Communication Association
McMaster University
Hamilton, ON L8B 4L9
Canada
(905) 525-9140
Web site: http://www.acc-cca.ca
The Canadian Communication Association promotes the study of
    communication issues among researchers, teachers, and stu-
    dents across Canada.

Goldwin-Meadow Laboratory
University of Chicago
5848 South University Avenue
Chicago, IL 60637
(773) 702-1562
Web site: http://goldin-meadow-lab.uchicago.edu
This laboratory at the University of Chicago's Department of Psychology is
    devoted to studying nonverbal communication, especially gestures.

International Society of Gesture Studies
Department of Communication Studies

University of Texas at Austin
1 University Station
Austin, TX 78712
(512) 471-5251
Web site: http://www.gesturestudies.com
This organization serves universities and colleges around the
     world that offer courses in the study of gestures.

McNeill Lab
Center for Gesture and Speech Research
University of Chicago
Green Hall
5848 South University Avenue
Chicago, IL 60637
(773) 702-8832
Web site: http://mcneilllab.uchicago.edu
This research center, headed by psychologist David McNeill,
     focuses on the relationship between thought and gestures.

National Communication Association
1765 N Street NW
Washington, DC 20036
(202) 464-4622
Web site: http://www.natcom.org
The National Communication Association promotes research into
     all forms of communication, including body language.

Robotics Institute
5000 Forbes Avenue
Pittsburgh, PA 15213
(412) 268-3818
Web site: http://www.ri.cmu.edu

The Robotics Institute applies research into nonverbal communication to create anthropomorphic (humanlike) robots.

SkillsUSA
14001 SkillsUSA Way
Leesburg, VA 20176
(703) 777-8810
Web site: http://www.skillsusa.org
SkillsUSA is a national organization that partners students, teachers, and employers to ensure a skilled and educated U.S. workforce.

Web Sites

Due to the changing nature of Internet links, Rosen Publishing has developed an online list of Web sites related to the subject of this book. This site is updated regularly. Please use this link to access the list:

http://www.rosenlinks.com/cwc/nverb

Boothman, Nicholas. *Convince Them in 90 Seconds or Less*. New York, NY: Workman Publishing, 2010.

Bowden, Mark. *Winning Body Language*. New York, NY: McGraw-Hill, 2010.

Brehove, Aaron. *Knack Body Language: Techniques on Interpreting Nonverbal Cues in the World and Workplace*. Guilford, CT: Knack, 2011.

Dimitrius, Jo-Ellan, and Wendy Patrick Mazzarella. *Reading People: How to Understand People and Predict Their Behavior—Anytime, Anyplace*. Rev. ed. New York, NY: Ballantine Books, 2008.

Driver, Janine, with Mariska van Aalst. *You Say More Than You Think*. New York, NY: Crown Publishers, 2010.

Ellsberg, Michael. *The Power of Eye Contact*. New York, NY: HarperPaperbacks, 2010.

Goman, Carol Kinsley. *The Nonverbal Advantage*. San Francisco, CA: Berrett-Koehler Publishers, 2008.

Hagen, Shelly. *The Everything Body Language Book*. Avon, MA: Adams Media, 2008.

Hartley, Gregory, and Maryann Karinch. *The Body Language Handbook*. Pompton Plains, NJ: Career Press, 2010.

Hartley, Gregory, and Maryann Karinch. *I Can Read You Like a Book*. Pompton Plains, NJ: Career Press, 2007.

Kuhnke, Elizabeth. *Body Language for Dummies*. Chichester, England: John Wiley & Sons, 2007.

Lambert, David. *Body Language 101*. New York, NY: Skyhorse Publishing, 2008.

Lieberman, David J. *You Can Read Anyone*. Lakewood, NJ: Viter Press, 2007.

Meyer, Pamela. *Liespotting: Proven Techniques to Detect Deception*. New York, NY: St. Martin's Press, 2010.

Navarro, Joe, and Marvin Karlins. *What Every Body Is Saying*. New York, NY: HarperCollins, 2008.

Navarro, Joe, and Toni Sciarra Poynter. *Louder Than Words*. New York, NY: HarperCollins, 2010.

Nierenberg, Gerard I., Henry H. Calero, and Gabriel Grayson. *How to Read a Person Like a Book*. Garden City Park, NY: Square One Publishers, 2009.

Pease, Allan, and Barbara Pease. *The Definitive Book of Body Language*. New York, NY: Bantam, 2006.

Reiman, Tonya. *The Power of Body Language*. New York, NY: Pocket Books, 2007.

Sayler, Sharon. *What Your Body Says and How to Master the Message*. Hoboken, NJ: John Wiley & Sons, 2010.

BIBLIOGRAPHY

Birdwhistell, Ray L. *Kinesics and Context: Essays on Body Motion Communication*. Philadelphia, PA: University of Pennsylvania Press, 1970.

Burgoon, Judee K., Laura K. Guerrero, and Kory Floyd. *Nonverbal Communication*. Boston, MA: Allyn & Bacon, 2009.

Eggert, Max A. *Brilliant Body Language*. Harlow, NY: Pearson Education, 2010.

Ekman, Paul. *Emotions Revealed*. 2nd ed. New York, NY: Holt, 2007.

Ekman, Paul. *Telling Lies*. 4th ed. New York, NY: W. W. Norton, 2009.

Ekman, Paul, and Erika L. Rosenberg, eds. *What the Face Reveals*. 2nd ed. New York, NY: Oxford University Press, 2005.

Furnham, Adrian, and Evgeniya Petrova. *Body Language in Business*. New York, NY: Palgrave Macmillan, 2010.

Givens, David B. *Your Body at Work: A Guide to Sight-Reading the Body Language of Business, Bosses, and Boardrooms*. New York, NY: St. Martin's Press, 2010.

Goman, Carol Kinsey. *The Silent Language of Leaders*. San Francisco, CA: Jossey-Bass, 2011.

Guerrero, Laura K., and Michael L. Hecht, eds. *The Nonverbal Communication Reader*. 3rd ed. Long Grove, IL: Waveland Press, 2007.

Hall, Edward T. *The Hidden Dimension*. Garden City, NY: Doubleday, 1966.

Harrigan, Jinni, Robert Rosenthal, and Klaus Scherer, eds. *The New Handbook of Methods of Nonverbal Behavior Research*. New York, NY: Oxford University Press, 2008.

Hogan, Kevin. *The Secret Language of Business*. Hoboken, NJ: John Wiley & Sons, 2008.

Ivy, Diana K., and Shawn T. Wahl. *The Nonverbal Self*. Boston, MA: Allyn & Bacon, 2008.

Knapp, Mark L., and Judith A. Hall. *Nonverbal Communication in Human Interaction*. 7th ed. Boston, MA: Wadsworth Publishing, 2009.

Manusov, Valerie, and Miles L. Patterson, eds. *The SAGE Handbook of Nonverbal Communication*. Thousand Oaks, CA: Sage Publications, 2006.

Mehrabian, Albert. *Nonverbal Communication*. Chicago, IL: Aldine-Atherton, 1972.

Remland, Martin S. *Nonverbal Communication in Everyday Life*. 3rd ed. Boston, MA: Allyn & Bacon, 2008.

Richmond, Virginia Peck, James C. McCroskey, and Mark L. Hickson. *Nonverbal Behavior in Interpersonal Relations*. 7th ed. Boston, MA: Allyn & Bacon, 2011.

Wharton, Tim. *Pragmatics and Non-Verbal Communication*. New York, NY: Cambridge University Press, 2009.